Introduction to the Book of Revelation

Introduction to the Book of Revelation

Worship, Witness and New Creation

under the supervision of
Dean Flemming

Theological Essentials

©Digital Theological Library 2025
Library of Congress Cataloging-in-Publication Data

Dean Flemming (creator).
Introduction to the Book of Revelation: Worship, Witness and New Creation / Dean Flemming
103 + x pp. cm. 12.7 x 20.32 (includes bibliography & map)
ISBN 979-8-89731-399-0 (Print)
ISBN 979-8-89731-150-7 (Ebook)
ISBN 979-8-89731-162-0 (Kindle)
ISBN 979-8-89731-166-8 (Abridged Audio Discussion)
  1. Bible. Revelation—Criticism, interpretation, etc.
  2. Bible. Revelation—Theology
BS2825.3 .F54 2025

Second Printing

This book is available in other languages at
www.DTLPress.com

Cover Image: "The Fall of Babylon" and "The Descent of the New Jerusalem" from the French *The Cloisters Apocalypse* (1330)
Image Credit: https://www.metmuseum.org

Contents

Series Preface
vii

Introduction
1

Chapter 1
Interpreting Revelation
5

Chapter 2
Historical and Cultural Context of Revelation
15

Chapter 3
Literary Genre and Structure
21

Chapter 4
Christ and the Churches
29

Chapter 5
Worship and the Lamb
35

Chapter 6
Judgment and Mercy
41

Chapter 7
The Church in Conflict
49

Chapter 8
The Multinational People of God
55

Chapter 9
Babylon the Great and the Fall of Empire
63

Chapter 10
The Return of the King
69

Chapter 11
A New Heaven and New Earth
75

Chapter 12
Some Leading Interpreters of Revelation
81

Chapter 13
Preaching and Teaching Revelation Today
89

Epilogue
Living Revelation Today
97

Selected Bibliography
99

Appendix
103

Series Preface

Artificial Intelligence (AI) is changing everything, including theological scholarship and education. This series, *Theological Essentials*, is designed to bring the creative potential of AI to the field of theological education. In the traditional model, a scholar with both mastery of the scholarly discourse and a record of successful classroom teaching would spend several months—or even several years—writing, revising and rewriting an introductory text which would then be transferred to a publisher who also invested months or years in production processes. Even though the end product was typically quite predictable, this slow and expensive process caused the prices of textbooks to balloon. As a result, students in developed nations paid more than they should have for the books and students in developing nations typically had no access to these (cost-prohibitive) textbooks until they appeared as discards and donations decades later. In previous generations, the need for quality assurance—in the form of content generation, expert review, copy-editing and printing time—may have made this slow, expensive and exclusionary approach inevitable. However, AI is changing everything.

This series is very different; it is created by AI. The cover of each volume identifies the work as "created under the supervision of" an expert in the field. However, that person is not an author in the traditional sense. The creator of each volume has been trained by the DTL staff in the use of AI and *the creator has used AI to create, edit, revise and recreate the text that you see*. With that creation process clearly identified, let me explain the goals of this series.

Our Goals:

Credibility: Although AI has made—and continues to make—huge strides over the last few years, no unsupervised AI can create a truly reliable or fully credible college or seminary level text. The limitations of AI generated content sometimes originates from the limitations of the content itself (the training set may be inadequate), but more often, user dissatisfaction with AI-generated content arises from human errors associated with poor prompt engineering. The DTL Press has sought to overcome both of these problems by hiring established scholars with widely recognized expertise to create books within their areas of expertise and by training those scholars and experts in AI prompt engineering. To be clear, the scholar whose name appears on the cover of this work has created this volume—generating, reading, regenerating, rereading and revising the work. Even though the work was generated (in varying degrees) by AI, the names of our scholarly creators appear on the cover as a guarantee that the content is equally credible with any introductory work which that scholar/creator would pen using the traditional model.

Stability: AI is generative, meaning that the response to each prompt is uniquely generated for that specific request. No two AI-generated responses are precisely the same. The inevitable variability of AI responses presents a significant pedagogical challenge for professors and students who wish to begin their discussions and analysis on the basis of a shared set of ideas. Educational institutions need stable texts in order to prevent pedagogical chaos. These books provide that stable text from which to teach, discuss and engage ideas.

Affordability: The DTL Press is committed to the idea that affordability should not be a barrier to knowledge. *All persons are equally deserving of the right to know and to understand.* Therefore, ebook versions of all DTL Press books are available from the DTL libraries without charge, and available as print books for a nominal fee. Our scholar/creators are to be thanked for their willingness to forego traditional royalty arrangements. (Our creators are compensated for their generative work, but they do not receive royalties in the traditional sense.)

Accessibility: The DTL Press would like to make high quality, low cost introductory textbooks available to everyone, everywhere in the world. The books in this series are immediately made available in multiple languages. The DTL Press will create translations in other languages upon request. Translations are, of course, generated by AI.

Our Acknowledged Limitations:

Some readers are undoubtedly thinking, "but AI can only produce derivative scholarship; AI can't create original, innovative scholarship." That criticism is, of course, largely accurate. AI is largely limited to aggregating, organizing and repackaging pre-existing ideas (although sometimes in ways that can be used to accelerate and refine the production of original scholarship). Still while acknowledging this inherent limitation of AI, the DTL Press would offer two comments: (1) Introductory texts are seldom meant to be truly ground breaking in their originality and (2) the DTL Press has other series dedicated to publishing original scholarship with traditional authorship.

Our Invitation:

The DTL Press would like to fundamentally reshape academic publishing in the theological world to make scholarship more accessible and more affordable in two ways. First, we would like to generate introductory texts in all areas of theological discourse, so that no one is ever forced to "buy a textbook" in any language. It is our vision for professors anywhere to be able to use one book, two books or an entire set of books in this series as the *introductory* textbooks for their classes. Second, we would also like to publish traditionally authored scholarly monographs for Open Access (free) distribution for an advanced scholarly readership.

Finally, the DTL Press is non-confessional and will publish works in any area of religious studies. Traditionally authored books are peer-reviewed; AI-generated introductory book creation is open to anyone with the required expertise to supervise content generation in that area of discourse. If you share the DTL Press's commitment to credibility, affordability and accessibility, contact us about changing the world of theological publishing by contributing to this series or a more traditionally authored series.

With high expectations,
Thomas E. Phillips
DTL Press Executive Director
www.thedtl.org
www.DTLpress.com

Introduction
The Reputation and Misuse of Revelation

The Book of Revelation occupies a unique — and often controversial — place in Christian imagination. Its rich symbolism, graphic imagery, and dramatic visions have fascinated and confounded readers for centuries. To some, Revelation is an inspired word of hope. To others, it is a source of fear and confusion. It has been both cherished as a powerful prophecy and avoided as an impenetrable mystery.

Unfortunately, Revelation has also been widely misused. In popular culture and pulpits alike, the book has often been reduced to speculative timelines, conspiracy theories, and fear-based eschatology. It has been deployed to justify violence, demonize political enemies, and escape present responsibilities in favor of apocalyptic sensationalism. These distortions not only betray the spirit of Revelation but also undermine its theological richness and pastoral power.

Revelation as Theological Scripture

Far from being a coded script about the end times, Revelation is deeply theological. It is a book of worship and witness, judgment and justice, conflict and communion. It presents a cosmic vision of God's reign through the crucified and risen Lamb, calling the church to follow him in faithful, sacrificial witness.

Revelation brings together rich biblical traditions—from the Hebrew prophets and wisdom literature to apocalyptic writings and Christological hymns. Its vision is not narrowly predictive but profoundly theological: a revealing of God's character, God's purposes in history, and God's promised future. The book draws us into the divine drama of redemption, inviting us to see the world not as empire sees it, but as God sees it.

The Book's Relevance in Contemporary Christian Life

Revelation continues to speak powerfully into the church's life across cultures and continents. In contexts of political repression, Revelation sustains communities of resistance. In situations of economic injustice, it unmasks the idolatry of Babylon. In settings of environmental crisis, it offers a vision of ecological renewal. And in places of apathy or compromise, it summons the church to prophetic fidelity.

Revelation is not merely about the end—it is about discipleship in the present, formed by the Lamb's vision of reality. The church is called to live now as a foretaste of the New Jerusalem, resisting the seductions of empire and bearing witness to the justice, mercy, and hope of God's reign.

The Flow and Purpose of This Book

This textbook is crafted for theological students across global contexts, aiming to equip them for thoughtful engagement with Revelation in both academic and pastoral settings. The chapters are arranged to move progressively from foundational tools of interpretation, to contextual and theological analysis, to practical application in ministry.

Chapter One explores interpretive methods and global perspectives to help readers approach the text responsibly. The subsequent chapters follow the book's unfolding narrative and theological themes: beginning with historical context and authorship, and proceeding through Christology, the letters to the churches, scenes of heavenly worship, the dynamics of judgment and mercy, the witness of the church, and Revelation's portrayal of empire and new creation.

Final chapters highlight leading interpreters, offer guidance on preaching and teaching Revelation, and encourage faithful application in local and global churches. Through it all, this book emphasizes Revelation's pastoral heart and its call to worship, resist, and hope in the Lamb who is and who is to come.

Chapter 1
Interpreting Revelation
Reading with Reverence and Wisdom

The Book of Revelation both invites and demands interpretation. It is arguably the most symbol-laden, misunderstood, and misused book in the Christian canon. Its evocative imagery — dragons and beasts, angels and plagues, thrones and judgments — has been the subject of endless fascination and frequent fear. Yet at its heart, Revelation is not a riddle to be solved but a revelation (*apokalypsis*): an unveiling of God's purposes in history, through the lens of Christ's victory and the Spirit's testimony to the churches.

Reading Revelation well requires wisdom, humility, and theological imagination. It is neither a literal forecast of headlines nor a cryptic manual for insiders. It is Scripture — pastoral, prophetic, and liturgical. As such, interpretation must be shaped by a commitment to the text's original context, the church's ongoing life, and the Spirit's voice in diverse communities around the world.

Four Classical Approaches to Reading Revelation

Throughout Christian history, interpreters have approached Revelation through four broad hermeneutical frameworks. These models — futurist, preterist, historicist, and idealist — are not exhaustive or mutually exclusive, but they reflect major tendencies in how Christians have sought to make sense of Revelation's strange and beautiful world.

Futurist Approach

The futurist view interprets most of Revelation (especially chapters 4–22) as referring to future, literal events that will occur at the end of history. Often associated with dispensational premillennialism, this approach became especially influential in North American evangelicalism during the 19th and 20th centuries. Through this lens, the book is read as a prophetic timetable outlining the Great Tribulation, rise of the Antichrist, and Second Coming of Christ.

This view stresses the sovereignty of God over history and highlights the hope of Christ's ultimate return. It has encouraged Christians to live with a sense of urgency and to anticipate God's final victory. However, it also carries serious pitfalls. When overly focused on predictive prophecy, the futurist approach can foster fear-based eschatology, unhealthy speculation, and even political complacency or fatalism. Such readings may attempt to match each symbol in Revelation with contemporary geopolitical events or figures, often resulting in distorted interpretations and misplaced theological priorities. In extreme forms, this approach reduces Revelation to an apocalyptic horoscope, undermining its theological richness and pastoral purpose.

Preterist Approach

The preterist approach views Revelation primarily as a message to the first-century churches under Roman rule. The beast symbolizes imperial persecution, and Babylon is seen as either Rome or apostate Jerusalem. Judgment scenes correspond to historical events such as the destruction of the temple in 70 CE.

Preterism rightly roots Revelation in its historical context and emphasizes the book's urgent relevance to its original audience. However, an overly restrictive preterism may mute the book's transhistorical theological power — its ongoing address to the church across ages and cultures.

Historicist Approach

The historicist reading understands Revelation as a panoramic overview of church history, from the apostolic age to the final consummation. Popular among Reformation-era Protestants, this view often identified the beast with the Roman Catholic papacy and Babylon with ecclesial corruption or political tyranny.

Though largely abandoned in scholarly circles today, historicist interpretations highlight how Revelation has long been a lens through which Christians have read their own times in light of God's purposes—sometimes wisely, sometimes dangerously.

Idealist (or Theological-Symbolic) Approach

The idealist or symbolic approach sees Revelation as a timeless theological vision depicting the cosmic conflict between good and evil, Christ and Satan, the church and empire. Rather than tying symbols to specific events or dates, this view emphasizes spiritual themes: God's sovereignty, the call to faithful witness, the judgment of evil, and the hope of new creation.

This approach foregrounds Revelation's liturgical, theological, and ethical dimensions, though it must avoid flattening the text into abstractions or ignoring its prophetic specificity.

Integrative and Theological Readings

In contemporary interpretation, few scholars or pastors adhere rigidly to just one approach. Many employ eclectic or integrative readings, combining insights from multiple models. For example, one might affirm that Revelation spoke directly to first-century churches (preterist), portrays enduring spiritual realities (idealist), and also anticipates the future consummation of God's kingdom (futurist).

Ultimately, reading Revelation well means treating it not as a puzzle to be solved, but as Scripture that shapes the church's vision, values, and vocation. This includes deep attentiveness to its Christ-centered focus, Trinitarian theology, symbolic coherence, and call to communal perseverance.

Reading with the Global Church

Revelation is not just interpreted — it is lived. Around the world, Christian communities have read the Apocalypse through the lens of their own suffering, struggle, and hope. These contextual interpretations reveal how the Spirit continues to speak through Revelation in profoundly relevant and transformative ways.

Liberation and Postcolonial Readings

In Latin America, Africa, and Asia, Revelation often has been embraced as a prophetic word to the oppressed. The imagery of beasts and Babylon is not abstract — it represents dictatorships, multinational corporations, and systems of poverty and racialized violence. In these settings, Revelation becomes a manual of resistance, calling the church to stand firm in the power of the Lamb and in solidarity with the marginalized.

Postcolonial interpreters emphasize that the Apocalypse critiques empire and idolatry, not merely ancient Rome, but all systems of domination. They challenge Western readings that ignore or sanitize this critique and call for a decolonized eschatology that sees the Lamb's reign as good news for the poor, not the powerful.

Ecological and Indigenous Perspectives

Revelation's visions of creation restored — the tree of life, the river of healing, and the renewal of the earth (Rev. 21–22) — resonate powerfully with Indigenous theologies and ecological ethics. In a time of global environmental crisis, these readings reclaim the Apocalypse as a text not of world-denial but earth-redemption.

Indigenous theologians lift up the importance of place, memory, and communal flourishing, viewing the New Jerusalem not as an escape from the world, but as a cosmic sanctuary of healed relationships — between peoples, lands, and God.

Feminist and Womanist Interpretations

Feminist readers of Revelation offer both critique and retrieval. They interrogate its gendered symbolism—noting how Babylon and the woman clothed with the sun represent competing ideals of femininity—and question readings that glorify divine violence or subordinate women's voices.

At the same time, feminist and womanist theologians recover Revelation's images of empowered witness and divine justice. Figures such as Elisabeth Schüssler Fiorenza, Barbara Rossing, and Catherine Keller show how the Apocalypse can be read as a vision of resistance and renewal, not as an endorsement of domination.

Interpreting Revelation's Symbols Responsibly

Revelation is steeped in symbol, allusion, and imagery. Locusts, trumpets, lampstands, scrolls, and thrones all function as theological signs rather than literal descriptions. To interpret the book responsibly, readers must attend to how symbols work, and how they connect to both biblical precedents and cultural context.

Symbols in Revelation are evocative and multivalent; they evoke emotion and prompt reflection. Yet they are also vulnerable to abuse. Literalistic or sensationalist readings can weaponize symbols, transforming images of divine justice into tools of fear or exclusion. Reading Revelation symbolically does not mean allegorizing away its meaning, but rather discerning how its visions function to reveal God's truth and invite transformed imagination.

Responsible interpretation requires a grounding in biblical intertextuality, cultural context, and theological humility. The goal is not to decode symbols into static referents, but to receive them as invitations to see reality differently.

Reading with Imagination

To read Revelation well is to read with sanctified imagination. The book's power lies not only in its doctrine but in its drama—its ability to awaken the senses, stir the spirit, and open readers to the mystery of God's cosmic purposes. Revelation does not provide a manual; it offers a vision. It is poetic prophecy, not prose exposition.

Reading with imagination means engaging Revelation's art, song, and metaphor as a way of entering into its theological world. The Lamb who reigns, the scroll that must be opened, the worship that never ends—these are images to be inhabited, not merely ideas to be explained. Through imagination, Revelation forms not only what the church believes, but how it sees, feels, hopes, and prays.

Such imaginative reading resists the reduction of Scripture to argument or timeline. It allows the Spirit to open new possibilities for understanding God's justice, presence, and future. In a world flattened by cynicism, Revelation calls the church to dream again.

Revelation as a Living Word

Revelation is not a text for private speculation but for public discipleship. Its images are meant to shape our imaginations, embolden our witness, and orient our hope. The church does not interpret Revelation from a place of neutrality—it does so as a community under pressure, navigating empire, longing for justice, and called to follow the Lamb wherever he goes (Rev. 14:4).

To read Revelation well, then, is not only an academic exercise—it is a form of spiritual formation. It demands of us what it demanded of John's churches: repentance, resilience, worship, and a willingness to see the world through heaven's eyes.

Questions for Reflection or Discussion
- Which of the four classical interpretive approaches to Revelation have shaped your own understanding of the book, and how might other approaches enrich or challenge your perspective?

- How can engagement with global and contextual interpretations of Revelation enrich the church's reading of Scripture?

Chapter 2
Historical and Cultural Context of Revelation

The Roman Empire and the Cult of Emperor Worship

To read Revelation faithfully, we must first immerse ourselves in the world that produced it — a world dominated by the Roman Empire. By the late first century CE, Rome had extended its influence across the Mediterranean basin, binding together diverse peoples under its rule through military conquest, administrative efficiency, and cultural assimilation. For many in the empire, Rome promised pax Romana — a "peace" secured by violence, taxation, and the suppression of dissent.

Central to this imperial project was the cult of emperor worship. While not uniform across the empire, the practice flourished particularly in Asia Minor, the region where the seven churches addressed in Revelation were located. Temples to the divine emperors stood prominently in cities like Pergamum and Ephesus. Inscriptions and public rituals honored emperors not merely as rulers but as semi-divine saviors and guarantors of prosperity. Participation in these practices was not merely a private matter of piety, but a public affirmation of loyalty to the empire.

For early Christians, this posed a profound dilemma. To refuse to participate in civic festivals or to decline to offer incense to Caesar could be seen as political subversion or even treason. In such a context, Revelation's repeated call to "overcome" takes on a sharply political dimension. It is a summons to fidelity amid pressure, not only from hostile outsiders but also from compromised insiders.

Social and Religious Landscape of Asia Minor

The seven churches addressed in Revelation (Rev. 2–3) were embedded in urban centers marked by Greco-Roman civic pride, economic complexity, and religious pluralism. Cities like Smyrna, Thyatira, and Laodicea were bustling centers of commerce and culture, connected by Roman roads and trade networks. Local guilds and associations often held feasts in honor of pagan deities, creating further tensions for Christians navigating social inclusion and spiritual integrity.

Religious life in Asia Minor was vibrant and deeply interconnected with politics and economics. Temples to Artemis, Apollo, Zeus, and the emperor himself shaped the religious skyline and civic identity. To reject these deities was to risk isolation, suspicion, and financial hardship. Thus, Revelation's condemnation of compromise—such as the rebukes against those who tolerate "Jezebel" (Rev. 2:20) or follow the teaching of "Balaam" (Rev. 2:14)—is not abstract but urgently contextual. The message confronts the cost of cultural assimilation.

Moreover, Jewish communities also formed part of this religious landscape. Revelation reflects tensions between some Christian and Jewish groups, particularly in cities where Christians were no longer protected under Judaism's legal status within the empire. The letter's sharp language toward "those who say they are Jews and are not" (Rev. 2:9; 3:9) must be handled with care, avoiding anti-Jewish interpretations. These passages reflect intra-communal conflict rather than blanket condemnation, and should be interpreted within the broader context of Roman persecution and identity negotiation.

Early Christian Communities and Resistance

Revelation is addressed not to a triumphant church but to vulnerable and varied communities. Some are experiencing persecution (Smyrna, Philadelphia), others are tempted toward accommodation (Pergamum, Thyatira), and still others are marked by complacency (Laodicea). These congregations are small, socially marginalized, and struggling to discern how to live as faithful followers of Jesus in a hostile world.

The book's original recipients were not insulated from Rome's power—they lived in its shadow daily. This explains Revelation's stark imagery: beasts, dragons, and prostitutes symbolize political and economic systems that oppress and seduce. For these believers, apocalyptic visions were not escapist fantasies but tools of resistance. The book provides them with a new map of reality—one in which the true King is not Caesar but the slain and risen Lamb.

In this context, Revelation functions as both a pastoral letter and a prophetic tract. It encourages the persecuted, warns the complacent, and reorients the imagination of the faithful. The call to "come out of Babylon" (Rev. 18:4) is not a retreat from society, but a radical reordering of allegiance. Christians are not to adopt imperial values but to bear witness to the Lamb—even if that witness leads to suffering.

Historical Interpretive Challenges

Understanding Revelation's historical setting is essential, but not without challenges. Was Revelation written during the reign of Nero (54–68 CE) or Domitian (81–96 CE)? While some argue for an earlier date due to references to persecution under Nero, most scholars favor the Domitianic period. By the late first century, the structures of emperor worship were more firmly established, and the church was increasingly viewed as a distinct and potentially subversive movement.

Additionally, interpreting symbolic language requires careful contextualization. "Babylon," for example, clearly alludes to Rome, echoing the Hebrew prophets' use of ancient Babylon as a symbol of oppressive empire. But Babylon also transcends Rome—it becomes a type of any system that dehumanizes, exploits, and resists the reign of God. In this way, the historical specificity of Revelation does not limit its relevance but expands its theological depth.

Scholars also continue to debate the extent and nature of persecution in Revelation's setting. While there is little evidence of widespread empire-wide persecution at this time, local hostilities, economic exclusion, and occasional violence likely created a climate of fear and instability. Revelation's message of hope, then, does not depend on dramatic martyrdoms but on everyday faithfulness.

Questions for Reflection or Discussion
- How does understanding the Roman imperial setting help clarify the meaning

and urgency of Revelation for its original readers?

- In what ways might the church today face temptations similar to those posed by Roman power and idolatry in the first century?

Chapter 3
Literary Genre and Structure

What Is an Apocalypse?

The Book of Revelation opens with a bold claim: it is "the revelation (Greek: apokalypsis) of Jesus Christ" (Rev. 1:1). This term signals that we are reading an apocalypse—a distinct genre of Jewish and early Christian literature that discloses divine mysteries, often through symbolic visions, heavenly journeys, and dualistic portrayals of good and evil. Far from predicting the future in coded detail, apocalyptic literature seeks to unveil the truth about the present from the perspective of heaven.

As a genre, apocalypse typically arises during periods of social crisis or political oppression. Its imagery speaks to those who live on the margins, offering assurance that what is seen is not all that is. Apocalyptic writing shifts the reader's vision—from the apparent power of earthly empires to the ultimate sovereignty of God. Thus, the purpose of Revelation is not to frighten or confuse, but to awaken and sustain hope.

Like other Jewish apocalypses (e.g., Daniel, 1 Enoch, 4 Ezra), Revelation shares common literary features: angelic mediators, symbolic numbers and creatures, cosmic conflict, and a climactic judgment followed by renewal. However, Revelation stands apart by merging apocalyptic vision with Christian proclamation centered on the crucified and risen Lamb. This theological distinctiveness makes Revelation both a continuation and a transformation of the apocalyptic tradition.

Revelation as Prophetic Literature

Revelation is not only an apocalypse—it explicitly identifies itself as prophecy (Rev. 1:3; 22:7, 10, 18–19). In the biblical tradition, prophets do more than foretell the future; they speak truth into the present, exposing injustice, calling for repentance, and revealing God's intentions. Like the prophets of Israel, John of Patmos proclaims judgment against unfaithfulness and hope for restoration.

What makes Revelation's prophecy distinctive is its Christocentric orientation. The message is rooted in the Lamb who was slain and who now reigns. The prophetic voice, therefore, is not merely moral exhortation or political critique—it is the voice of the risen Christ, calling the churches to faithful endurance in a hostile world. John's prophetic vision draws its energy from

Scripture's past, speaks directly to his contemporary audience, and opens a theological horizon that embraces all nations.

In this way, Revelation functions as pastoral prophecy. It challenges complacent believers, comforts the afflicted, and re-centers the community's imagination on God's sovereignty and the Lamb's sacrificial victory. Its prophetic power lies not in predicting dates but in naming idols, resisting empire, and nurturing worship that aligns with God's reign.

Letter Form and Pastoral Intent

In addition to being an apocalypse and prophecy, Revelation is also a letter—a circular letter addressed to seven historical churches in Asia Minor (Rev. 2–3). The opening salutation (Rev. 1:4–5) follows the standard epistolary format of the time, signaling that this book is meant to be read aloud in congregational settings.

As a letter, Revelation is profoundly pastoral. It engages with real communities, each facing distinct struggles: persecution, compromise, materialism, fear, and spiritual apathy. The messages to the seven churches are contextualized mini-sermons—offering praise, correction, warning, and promise. But the number seven also carries symbolic weight: it represents fullness or completeness. In this way, the letter is also addressed to the entire church across time and place.

The pastoral dimension of Revelation is often missed amid its vivid visions. But when read as a letter, the text's urgency and intimacy come into focus. The risen Christ speaks not from a distant future but in the midst of the church's present circumstances. This pastoral concern challenges interpretations that treat Revelation as a detached eschatological puzzle, rather than as God's word to living communities.

Revelation as Rhetoric

In addition to its apocalyptic symbolism and theological depth, Revelation is a deeply rhetorical text. John writes not simply to inform but to persuade, provoke, and form a faithful community under pressure. His language is intentionally vivid and dramatic, employing irony, contrast, repetition, and escalating imagery to engage the imagination and stir emotional response. The goal is not detached analysis but transformational encounter. John seeks to awaken his readers — to jolt them out of complacency, expose the seductive power of empire, and embolden them to follow the Lamb in costly witness. Recognizing Revelation as rhetoric invites interpreters to consider not just what the text says, but how it seeks to move its audience. This rhetorical power has resonated across cultures, particularly in communities facing persecution or injustice, where Revelation's urgent call to perseverance and hope is not abstract but existentially real.

Authorship
Who Was "John of Patmos"?

The text identifies its author simply as "John" (Rev. 1:1, 4, 9; 22:8) — a prophet and visionary who receives this revelation while exiled on the island of Patmos "on account of the word of God and the testimony of Jesus" (Rev. 1:9). But who exactly is this John?

Some early church traditions (e.g., Justin Martyr, Irenaeus) associate him with John the Apostle, the beloved disciple of Jesus. Others have argued for John the Elder, a separate church leader referenced by Papias. Modern scholarship remains divided. Most agree that Revelation's highly distinctive Greek style, theological themes, and genre make it unlikely to have been written by the same author as the Gospel of John. Today, the majority view sees "John of Patmos" as a Christian prophet — likely of Jewish background, deeply immersed in Scripture, and a pastoral leader known to the seven churches.

Importantly, John does not write as a detached scribe or abstract theologian. He identifies himself as a "servant," a "brother," and a "partner in the tribulation and the kingdom" (Rev. 1:1, 9). His authority derives not from his status but from his faithfulness to Christ amid suffering. This humility is essential to Revelation's ethos: its visions are not elitist revelations for the few, but communal messages rooted in solidarity, suffering, and hope.

Literary Patterns and Narrative Flow

Though its symbolism may appear chaotic at first glance, Revelation is intricately structured. It follows a carefully designed narrative arc, rich with literary symmetry, repetition, and theological coherence.

At a macro level, the book can be divided as follows:

Prologue and Vision of Christ (1:1–20)
Messages to the Seven Churches (2:1–3:22)
Heavenly Throne Room and the Scroll (4:1–5:14)
3 Cycles of Judgment (Seals, Trumpets, Bowls 6–16)
Conflict and Fall of Babylon (17–18)
Victory of the Lamb and the Final Judgment (19–20)
New Creation and Epilogue (21–22)

These cycles are not linear but recursive — they revisit the same themes from different angles, intensifying their impact. Each series (seals, trumpets, bowls) builds on the last, often ending in glimpses of worship, judgment, or salvation. Interludes offer pastoral pauses, reminding readers of God's protection and purpose.

The book is also full of numerical and structural symbolism: sevens, twelves, and multiples thereof are used to signify completeness, authority, and divine order. The repetition of hymns, the rhythm of interludes, and the careful placement of visions show that Revelation is not random, but liturgically and theologically orchestrated.

Interpreting Revelation's structure is not merely academic—it shapes how we understand its message. When we see the Lamb enthroned at the center of the narrative, the entire book reorients around the theology of redemptive suffering, worship, and witness.

Questions for Reflection or Discussion

- How does recognizing Revelation as a combination of apocalypse, prophecy, and letter shape your reading of the text?
- What role does Revelation's symbolic language play in challenging or inspiring your theological imagination?

Chapter 4
Christ and the Churches

The Vision of the Glorified Christ

Revelation begins not with beasts or battles but with a vision of Christ—a majestic, risen figure who walks among the lampstands (Rev. 1:9-20). John, exiled on the island of Patmos, is "in the Spirit" on the Lord's Day when he hears a voice "like a trumpet" and turns to see one "like a Son of Man" (1:10, 13). What follows is one of the most awe-inspiring depictions of Jesus in all of Scripture.

This vision fuses Old Testament imagery: the white hair of the Ancient of Days (Dan. 7:9), the flaming eyes of divine scrutiny (Dan. 10:6), the sword from the mouth symbolizing the power of the Word (Isa. 11:4), and the seven stars representing the angels or spirits of the churches. This is not a gentle portrait of Jesus meek and mild—it is the cosmic Christ, exalted yet present, radiant with glory and terrifying in holiness.

Yet this transcendent Christ is also intimately connected with his people. He walks among the lampstands, which represent the churches. He holds their "angels" in his right hand, guarding and guiding them. This duality—

transcendence and immanence, majesty and presence—establishes the tone for the rest of Revelation. The Lord of glory is also the pastor of struggling congregations. He is not aloof, but lovingly involved in the life of the church.

This Christ is not only the Lamb who was slain (Rev. 5:6), but the high priest who examines, cleanses, and intercedes for his people. His presence is both comforting and convicting. He is the one who sees the churches for who they truly are—and who calls them to become who they are meant to be.

Seven Churches, Seven Realities

Revelation 2–3 contains personal, pastoral messages to seven churches in Asia Minor: Ephesus, Smyrna, Pergamum, Thyatira, Sardis, Philadelphia, and Laodicea. These were real communities facing real challenges—external persecution, internal compromise, economic hardship, and spiritual apathy. But, as noted earlier, the number seven, a symbol of completeness, signals that these messages are meant for the whole church in all locations and generations.

Each message follows a similar structure: an introduction of Christ (drawing from the vision in chapter 1), praise or rebuke, exhortation, and promise. But each message is tailored to the specific context of that church:

- Ephesus is praised for its orthodoxy but rebuked for losing its "first love."
- Smyrna, facing persecution, is encouraged to remain faithful even unto death.
- Pergamum is commended for holding fast but warned against tolerating false teaching.
- Thyatira excels in love and service but is dangerously tolerant of moral compromise.
- Sardis has a reputation for life but is, in truth, spiritually dead.
- Philadelphia is weak but faithful and is given an open door.
- Laodicea is wealthy and self-satisfied but called out for being lukewarm and blind.

These portraits are both diagnostic and prophetic. They unveil the inner life of each community, revealing strengths and vulnerabilities. At the same time, they call the churches into a deeper fidelity to Christ and his kingdom. Each message ends with the refrain: "Let anyone who has an ear listen to what the Spirit is saying to the churches" (Rev. 2:7, etc.). The call is collective and ongoing.

Globally, churches today can find their own stories reflected in these seven. Some suffer like Smyrna. Others may resemble Laodicea, content in material wealth but spiritually impoverished. Others, like Philadelphia, may feel small and marginalized but remain true. Revelation insists that Christ knows each one intimately and speaks into their context with precision and compassion.

Commendation, Rebuke, and Call to Overcome

The messages to the churches are not generic affirmations or condemnations—they are marked by theological nuance and pastoral care. Christ offers commendation where faithfulness is evident, such as in Smyrna and Philadelphia. He gives rebuke where compromise or complacency has taken root, as in Sardis and Laodicea. But in every case, there is a call to overcome (*nikaō*)—a summons to spiritual resilience, covenant loyalty, and missional perseverance.

To "overcome" does not mean to dominate others, but to remain faithful as Christ did. In fact, Revelation links overcoming with the Lamb's own victory (Rev. 3:21; 5:5). The conquerors are those who do not yield to fear, idolatry, or imperial pressures. They are those who, like Jesus, endure suffering in hope and resist the powers that would seduce or destroy them.

The promises to the overcomers are breathtaking: access to the tree of life, protection from the second death, a white stone with a new name, authority over the nations, and a place in God's eternal city. These are not escape routes from history but eschatological affirmations of those who live faithfully within it. They cast vision for a discipleship that is costly yet crowned.

Hearing the Spirit
Contextual and Global Applications

In every message to the churches, the Spirit speaks. This reinforces the living and ongoing nature of Revelation's call. These are not static letters but dynamic words addressed to every generation of believers. To hear the Spirit today is to attend to both Scripture and context—to listen for the Word of Christ in our own time.

Across the globe, Revelation 2-3 continues to speak in varied ways. In places where the church is persecuted—such as parts of North Africa, East Asia, or the Middle East—the promise to Smyrna resonates deeply. In areas marked by economic affluence and consumerism, such as much of the West, the critique of Laodicea cuts close. In Indigenous and postcolonial contexts, the warning against cultural assimilation echoes the challenge faced by Pergamum and Thyatira.

Interpreters from the global South have highlighted how Revelation affirms the marginalized and critiques systems of wealth and domination. Feminist readers have emphasized

Christ's rebuke of Jezebel not as a condemnation of women's leadership, but as a critique of idolatrous teachings that lead others astray—calling for discernment without scapegoating. Charismatic and Pentecostal traditions have underscored the role of the Spirit and the prophetic call to faithfulness amid trials.

The central theme is clear: Christ knows the churches. He walks among them, sees them, speaks to them. And he invites them not to fear, but to listen—to repent, to endure, and to follow him.

Questions for Reflection or Discussion
- What aspects of Christ's identity in Revelation challenge or deepen your understanding of who Jesus is?
- How do the messages to the seven churches speak prophetically to churches across cultures today?
- Which of the seven churches most closely resembles your current faith community, and why?

Chapter 5
Worship and the Lamb

The Throne Room Vision

After the personal messages to the churches in Revelation 2–3, John is invited to "come up here" (Rev. 4:1), signaling a dramatic shift in perspective. What unfolds in chapters 4 and 5 is not simply a change in scenery—it is a theological reorientation. John is drawn into the throne room of heaven, where he beholds the worship of the One seated on the throne. This vision is the spiritual and liturgical center of Revelation. Everything that follows will flow from and return to this central revelation of God's sovereignty and the Lamb's worthiness.

John's description is both majestic and mysterious. The throne is encircled by rainbow-like light, evoking the covenant with Noah (Gen. 9), and surrounded by twenty-four elders, likely representing the twelve tribes of Israel and the twelve apostles—God's people in fullness. Four living creatures, drawn from the visions of Ezekiel and Isaiah, symbolize all creation and ceaselessly proclaim, "Holy, holy, holy, the Lord God the Almighty" (Rev. 4:8).

This scene of heavenly worship is not disconnected from earthly realities. It is a theological counter-narrative to the emperor's throne in Rome. While the empire proclaims Caesar as "lord and god," Revelation unveils the true source of authority. Worship in Revelation is deeply political—it reorients allegiance away from the powers of the world and toward the holy Creator.

The repeated emphasis on God as "the one who was and is and is to come" (Rev. 4:8) reminds us that divine sovereignty is not contingent on present circumstances. This is a word of assurance for marginalized believers then and now: the throne is occupied, and history is not spinning out of control.

Worthy Is the Lamb
Victory Through Sacrifice

Chapter 5 deepens and personalizes the vision. A sealed scroll—likely symbolizing God's redemptive plan—is introduced, and a question rings out: "Who is worthy to open the scroll?" (Rev. 5:2). No one in heaven or earth is found worthy—until the Lamb appears.

The Lamb is introduced with paradoxical imagery: he is the "Lion of the tribe of Judah" (5:5), evoking royal power, but when John turns, he sees not a lion, but a Lamb standing as if it had been slain (5:6). This visual reversal is the theological core of Revelation. Power is redefined through vulnerability. Victory is achieved not through domination, but through self-giving love.

This moment also introduces a pattern that recurs throughout Revelation: what John hears and what he sees are in tension, and their juxtaposition reveals a deeper theological truth. He hears of a lion but sees a lamb; he hears 144,000 but sees a great multitude (Rev. 7:4, 9). These contrasts invite the reader to move beyond surface expectations and to see through the lens of God's unexpected ways.

The Lamb bears marks of sacrifice but also possesses "seven horns and seven eyes" — symbols of perfect power and divine insight. He is not weak, but his strength is cruciform. This is the paradox of Christian theology: the slain Lamb is the sovereign Lord.

Once the Lamb takes the scroll, heaven erupts in worship. A new song is sung:

> You are worthy... for you were slaughtered and by your blood you ransomed for God saints from every tribe and language and people and nation (Rev. 5:9).

Here, redemption is not abstract — it is global and inclusive. The church is not defined by ethnicity or geography but by worshipful allegiance to the Lamb. This has profound implications for ecclesiology, mission, and inter-cultural dialogue.

Worship as Political Resistance

Worship in Revelation is never neutral. In the Roman world, to worship Christ was to refuse to worship Caesar, and this had real consequences: economic exclusion, social shaming, and even death. Revelation's vision of the throne room offers a subversive liturgy. It insists that ultimate loyalty belongs to God and the Lamb, not to any human empire or idol.

This kind of worship forms a different kind of community. It shapes people who resist Babylon's seduction, who endure suffering for the sake of the gospel, and who embody the values of the coming kingdom. Worship becomes a form of resistance, a rehearsal for the reign of God, and a witness to a different order of power.

Throughout history, oppressed communities have drawn strength from this vision. Enslaved Africans in the Americas, singing spirituals about the coming deliverance; Indigenous Christians preserving their culture while professing faith in Christ; believers in authoritarian regimes gathering in secret — all have found in Revelation 4–5 a vision of divine justice and dignity that transcends human tyranny.

The Lamb-shaped throne also challenges triumphalist or nationalistic Christianity. The Lamb does not conquer like Caesar. He reigns through love, not coercion. True worship invites transformation—not just of emotion, but of allegiance, ethics, and imagination.

Liturgy and Mission in Revelation

Revelation 4-5 is filled with liturgical language: hymns, antiphons, doxologies, and symbolic actions. These scenes have shaped the worship life of the global church—from Orthodox liturgies to Pentecostal praise gatherings. But Revelation's worship is never escapist. It sends the worshiper back into the world with new eyes and a new calling.

Worship in Revelation is missional. The Lamb "has made them to be a kingdom and priests serving our God, and they will reign on earth" (Rev. 5:10). The people of God are not passive spectators but active participants in God's redemptive plan. Worship forms a priestly people, empowered to bear witness, practice justice, and proclaim good news.

Global theological voices have emphasized this dynamic. African theologians, for instance, highlight how worship includes lament, protest, and the longing for liberation. Asian theologians point to worship as a space of healing and cosmic harmony. Latin American theologians connect worship with economic justice and political accountability. These perspectives deepen our understanding of Revelation's vision—not as a private spiritual high, but as the heartbeat of public discipleship.

Questions for Reflection or Discussion

- How might Revelation's picture of the slaughtered Lamb, who conquers not by force or violence but by self-giving love challenge common ways of thinking and living in your context?
- In what ways can worship today function as a form of resistance to injustice, idolatry, or cultural conformity, as it does in Revelation?
- How might your own church's worship practices more fully reflect the global, inclusive vision of redeemed community in Revelation 5:9–10?

Chapter 6
Judgment and Mercy
The Seals, Trumpets, and Bowls

The Seven Seals
Suffering and Sovereignty

Revelation's dramatic vision of judgment begins when the Lamb opens the first of seven seals on the scroll introduced in chapter 5. Each seal unveils a new dimension of human and cosmic crisis. The first four seals unleash the infamous Four Horsemen of the Apocalypse (Rev. 6:1–8), representing conquest, war, economic injustice, and death. These images are not futuristic predictions but present realities — refracted through theological imagination. They reflect what happens when human power runs unchecked and idolatrous systems go unchallenged.

Importantly, it is the Lamb who opens the seals. This detail underscores a crucial truth: the suffering of the world is not outside God's knowledge or redemptive plan. Even amid chaos, the scroll remains in the Lamb's hands. This does not mean God causes suffering, but that suffering is neither random nor sovereign.

The fifth seal shifts focus to "the souls of those who had been slain for the word of God" (Rev. 6:9). They cry out, "How long?"—a lament that echoes through Scripture (cf. Ps. 13:1; Hab. 1:2). The presence of lament in Revelation reminds us that honest suffering belongs within the realm of faith. God does not silence the cry for justice; rather, it is heard, affirmed, and answered in time.

The sixth seal unleashes cosmic upheaval—earthquakes, darkened skies, a shaking of the created order. Yet before the seventh seal is opened, a dramatic pause unfolds.

The Interludes
Divine Patience and the Sealed Saints

Between the sixth and seventh seals comes an interlude (Rev. 7) that offers a vision of divine mercy and protection. John hears the number of the sealed—144,000 from the tribes of Israel—but then he sees a "great multitude that no one could count, from every nation, tribe, people and language" (7:9). This is another example of Revelation's hear/see dynamic (cf. 5:5–6): what John hears (a limited, symbolic number) contrasts with what he sees (an expansive, inclusive vision).

This global multitude stands not in fear, but in worship. They wear white robes and hold palm branches, signs of victory and joy. They have come through "the great tribulation" (7:14), not by avoiding suffering, but by remaining faithful through it. They are not spectators but participants in God's redemptive drama.

These interludes are crucial. They remind readers that judgment is never God's final word. Mercy, mission, and the sealing of God's people stand at the center of the apocalyptic drama. Even amid devastation, God protects, remembers, and redeems.

The Seven Trumpets
Wake-Up Calls to the World

When the seventh seal is opened, silence fills heaven for half an hour (8:1) — a sacred pause before the next sequence. Then comes the blowing of seven trumpets, which announce plagues and disasters reminiscent of the Exodus story: hail and fire, poisoned waters, darkness, and locusts. These judgments intensify the narrative and underscore Revelation's continuity with biblical prophecy.

Trumpets in Scripture are warning signals, calls to attention (Joel 2:1; Zeph. 1:14–16). In Revelation, they function as wake-up calls to a world asleep to injustice and idolatry. They are not arbitrary acts of destruction, but divine summonses to repentance. The repeated pattern — partial devastation (often affecting a third of creation) — signals that these are judgments held in check, designed to provoke moral reflection rather than annihilation.

However, Revelation is painfully honest: "The rest of humankind… did not repent" (Rev. 9:20-21). This tragic refrain reveals that judgment alone does not transform hearts. Yet even here, God's purpose is not abandonment. The next interlude (Rev. 10-11) introduces the prophetic witness of God's people.

The Role of the Witnesses and the Seventh Trumpet

Before the seventh trumpet sounds, John is given another vision that shifts the focus from cosmic events to earthly vocation. A mighty angel descends with a little scroll (Rev. 10), which John must eat—a symbol of internalizing God's word in order to proclaim it. Then comes the introduction of two prophetic witnesses (Rev. 11), who prophesy, and suffer, and are ultimately vindicated by God.

These witnesses are clothed in sackcloth, echoing the biblical prophets of old. Their ministry lasts 1,260 days—a symbolic period often associated with suffering and tribulation (cf. Dan. 7:25; Rev. 12:6). They call people to repentance, perform signs, and stand as living embodiments of truth. Eventually, they are killed by "the beast that rises from the bottomless pit" (11:7), their bodies left in the street as a mockery. But after three and a half days, the breath of life enters them, and they are raised and taken into heaven before the eyes of their enemies (11:11-12).

The two witnesses have been variously interpreted—as individuals, symbolic representations of the church, or the Law and the Prophets. But within the narrative logic of Revelation, they most clearly represent the faithful, prophetic church in mission: those who bear witness to the Lamb in word and deed, often at great cost.

Their story is not tragic but triumphant. In their death and resurrection, they mirror the path of Christ. Their witness is vindicated not through power, but through faithfulness. Revelation redefines victory through the pattern of the cross and resurrection, a model of witness that speaks prophetically into every age.

This vision anchors Revelation's theology of judgment in a theology of witness. The church is not a passive observer but a prophetic participant in God's redemptive work—a theme that will be explored more fully in the following chapter.

When the seventh trumpet finally sounds, it announces not more destruction but celebration:

> The kingdom of the world has become the kingdom of our Lord and of his Messiah, and he will reign forever and ever (Rev. 11:15).

Here, judgment gives way to consummation. What was partial becomes full. Heaven rejoices not in ruin, but in redemption.

The Seven Bowls
Final Wrath and Final Mercy

The final judgment sequence comes in the form of seven bowls (Rev. 15–16). These are poured out in rapid succession, echoing the plagues of Egypt and drawing attention to the stubbornness of human hearts. The language here is intense: painful sores, blood in rivers, scorching heat, darkness, and earthquake. Unlike the earlier trumpets, these bowls affect the whole of creation. Yet even here, the aim is not vindictiveness but truth-telling. Evil is exposed, and its consequences laid bare.

Crucially, before the bowls are poured out, those who "conquered the beast" are seen standing by the sea, singing the song of Moses and the Lamb (Rev. 15:2–3). This is a liturgical interlude, mirroring Israel's song after deliverance at the Red Sea. It reminds us that God's justice is not arbitrary — it is rooted in liberation history and aims toward healing.

Even the harshest judgments in Revelation point toward restoration, not obliteration. God's wrath is God's "yes" to the victims of violence, exploitation, and deceit. It is the response of holy love to a world that refuses to repent. But the final goal is not destruction—it is new creation, as will be revealed in the chapters ahead.

Questions for Reflection or Discussion

- How can the interplay of judgment and mercy in Revelation shape a more hopeful and responsible theology of divine justice?
- In what ways might your own cultural context influence how you perceive the themes of wrath and redemption?
- What does Revelation teach us about the nature of Christian witness in times of opposition or political pressure?
- How might the church in the Western world recover its prophetic voice in light of Revelation's call to bear faithful witness?

Chapter 7
The Church in Conflict
The Dragon and the Beasts

The Cosmic Battle and the Woman/Dragon Narrative

In Revelation 12, the apocalyptic spotlight turns from heavenly worship and prophetic witness to a cosmic conflict between the forces of good and evil. At the center of this vision is a woman clothed with the sun, who gives birth to a child destined "to rule all the nations" (12:5). Opposing her is a great red dragon, representing "that ancient serpent, who is called the Devil and Satan" (12:9). This dramatic scene blends mythic and theological motifs, evoking Genesis 3, messianic hope, and ancient Near Eastern combat imagery.

The woman likely symbolizes the faithful people of God—Israel and the church—through whom the Messiah comes into the world. The dragon seeks to devour the child, but the child is caught up to God, and the woman flees into the wilderness, where she is divinely nourished (12:6). This wilderness is not abandonment but preservation—a place where the church endures, sustained by grace.

The child's ascension echoes Jesus' resurrection and exaltation, marking the dragon's defeat in heaven. Yet this victory leads to intensified conflict on earth:

> Then the dragon was angry... and went off to make war on the rest of her children, those who keep the commandments of God and hold the testimony of Jesus (12:17).

This framing of spiritual warfare is essential to Revelation. The persecution of the church is not merely sociopolitical—it is cosmic. The dragon wages war not just with individuals but with the faithful community. Yet the church is not helpless. Believers overcome "by the blood of the Lamb and by the word of their testimony" (12:11). The Lamb's victory reshapes the battle, and the church resists not with violence, but with faithfulness.

The Identity of the Beasts and Their Power

In Revelation 13, the dragon summons two beasts—one from the sea and one from the earth—to carry out his work. These beasts are not mere monsters of fantasy; they are symbolic representations of political and religious power systems that oppose God's reign.

The first beast, rising from the sea, resembles the composite beasts of Daniel 7. It receives authority from the dragon, demands worship, and blasphemes God. It represents imperial political power, likely a veiled reference to the Roman Empire but also a paradigm for all empires that deify themselves. The beast's "wounded head" that seemed to recover (13:3) may allude to the Nero redivivus myth, suggesting a regime that claims invincibility, even resurrection-like authority.

The second beast, arising from the earth, appears gentle—like a lamb—but speaks like a dragon. This beast performs signs, enforces worship of the first beast, and controls economic life by requiring a mark on the hand or forehead. This mark, associated with the infamous number 666, is often misunderstood. Rather than a microchip or bar code, it likely symbolizes compulsory allegiance to empire—a counterfeit to the sealing of God's servants in chapter 7. This beast represents ideological or religious systems that legitimize and enforce oppressive political power.

Together, the two beasts form a counterfeit trinity with the dragon—a satanic parody of God, Christ, and Spirit. They mimic divine power, demand worship, and enslave through deception. Revelation unmasks these systems and calls the church to discernment.

Deception, Idolatry, and Economic Control

Revelation 13 emphasizes that the beasts do not rule through brute force alone—they also operate through deception, spectacle, and control. The second beast performs signs to lead people astray. The first beast dazzles with its resilience and power. Together, they create a world in which compromise seems rational and resistance seems futile.

Economic control plays a key role. The beast's mark determines who can "buy or sell" (13:17), making faithfulness not just a spiritual decision but a costly one. In ancient Asia Minor, Christians who refused to participate in emperor worship or trade guild rites risked social isolation and economic hardship. In many modern contexts, Christians still face similar pressures—from corrupt governments, predatory economies, or state-aligned religious systems.

Revelation reveals that the greatest threat to the church is not always persecution—it is seduction. The beasts promise peace, security, and prosperity, but they demand allegiance to lies. The call of Revelation is to resist idolatry in all its forms, even when it wears the mask of religion or patriotism.

The Endurance and Wisdom of the Saints

In the face of this overwhelming evil, Revelation offers neither escapism nor despair. Instead, it calls for endurance and wisdom:

> This calls for patient endurance and faithfulness on the part of the saints (13:10).
> This calls for wisdom (13:18).

Endurance (*hypomonē*) is not passive waiting—it is active resistance sustained by hope. Wisdom (*sophia*) is not esoteric knowledge—it is spiritual discernment grounded in the fear of God. The faithful are called to recognize the beasts for what they are and to refuse their mark, even when the cost is high.

This is the vocation of the church in every generation. From underground house churches in China, to Indigenous congregations resisting cultural erasure, to urban Christians navigating political idolatry in the West, Revelation invites communities to recognize when the powers of this world are playing God—and to stand firm.

Questions for Reflection or Discussion

- In what ways does Revelation 12–13 reshape your understanding of spiritual warfare as both cosmic and political? How does this affect the church's mission today?
- How do the "beasts" in your own cultural or national context attempt to win allegiance—

whether through power, spectacle, ideology, or economic control?
- What might it mean for the church to resist the Beast in you cultural context?

Chapter 8
The Multinational People of God

The 144,000 and the Great Multitude (Rev. 7)

In Revelation 7, after the opening of the sixth seal and before the seventh, John is given a vision of God's people, presented in two strikingly different but theologically connected images. First, he hears the number of those sealed: 144,000 from the twelve tribes of Israel. Then, he turns and sees a great multitude that no one could count, from every nation, tribe, people, and language (7:4, 9).

This hear-see pattern (introduced in Rev. 5:5–6) signals an apocalyptic paradox: what John hears is not what he sees, yet both are necessary for understanding. The 144,000 is a symbolic number, representing the fullness and completeness of God's covenant people. It draws from the imagery of ancient Israel, indicating a people set apart and sealed for protection. But the great multitude reveals the scope of that people—not ethnically homogenous but gloriously diverse, gathered from all corners of the earth.

Theologically, these visions affirm that the church is both rooted in the story of Israel and radically expanded through the mission of the

Lamb. The people of God are not defined by ethnicity, nationality, or geography but by their allegiance to Jesus Christ. This is a community shaped by grace, marked by endurance, and united in worship.

Faithfulness and Martyrdom

This great multitude is not merely a worshiping assembly; they are also a faithful and suffering people. They have "come out of the great tribulation" (Rev. 7:14). Their white robes are not tokens of privilege but signs of perseverance. They have washed their robes "in the blood of the Lamb"—a paradoxical image that reveals the cost of discipleship and the source of cleansing.

In Revelation, martyrdom is not an anomaly but a normative expectation for those who follow the Lamb. These saints are not exceptional heroes but ordinary believers who have remained faithful amid trials. Their victory lies not in escaping suffering but in bearing witness through it. They are the "servants of our God" (7:3), those who carry the testimony of Jesus wherever they go.

Their posture—standing, not bowed—indicates vindication. Their palm branches evoke the imagery of festal processions and joyful deliverance. Their song is not self-congratulatory but centered on "salvation belonging to our God…

and to the Lamb" (7:10). This is the identity of the church: redeemed, worshiping, and witness-bearing in the face of adversity.

The Redeemed with the Lamb on Mount Zion (Rev. 14:1–5)

A second vision of the 144,000 appears in Revelation 14. This time, they are not seen in suffering but in triumph: standing with the Lamb on Mount Zion. This image reverses the scenes of oppression and idolatry in the previous chapter (Rev. 13), where the beast is worshiped and his name marked on followers. Here, the Lamb's followers are marked by his name and his Father's name on their foreheads (14:1).

The 144,000 sing a new song—a song only they can learn, suggesting an intimacy with the Lamb forged through shared suffering and loyalty. They are described as "blameless," as those who "follow the Lamb wherever he goes" (14:4–5). This language evokes discipleship, chastity, and covenantal integrity.

Importantly, this group is not defined by triumphalism but by their refusal to compromise with the world's idolatrous systems. In contrast to Babylon's seductions, these are a counter-community of integrity, purity, and worship. They stand on Mount Zion, not in escape from the world, but as the firstfruits of a redeemed creation.

This image of the church completes the identity begun in Revelation 7: the people of God are not only sealed and saved—they are also singing, standing, and following. Their lives are marked by moral distinction, not moral superiority; by humble devotion, not domination.

The Sea of Glass and the Song of the Redeemed (Rev. 15:2–4)

A third vision of the faithful appears in Revelation 15, just before the final bowl judgments. Here, those who "conquered the beast and its image and the number of its name" stand beside a sea of glass mixed with fire—a place of both transcendence and testing (15:2). They hold harps of God and sing "the song of Moses…and the song of the Lamb" (15:3).

This liturgical moment links exodus and redemption—Moses and the Lamb. Just as Israel was delivered from Pharaoh, so now the redeemed celebrate deliverance from Babylon and the beast. Their song praises God's justice and truth, echoing the Psalms and Exodus 15:

> Great and amazing are your deeds… Just and true are your ways, King of the nations (15:3).

This vision emphasizes that the church's identity is formed through worship and memory. The faithful are those who not only resist the beast but remember God's saving acts. They do not sing generic hymns—they sing songs grounded in history and hope, shaped by God's justice and the Lamb's mercy. Their worship becomes a prophetic declaration of God's coming reign over all nations.

The Church's Identity and Global Mission

These images—from the multitude, to the sealed, to the singers on Mount Zion—together present a profound portrait of the church: diverse, faithful, global, and missional. The redeemed are gathered "from every nation, tribe, people, and language"—a phrase repeated throughout the book (5:9; 7:9; 14:6). This refrain reinforces the inclusivity of the gospel and the expansiveness of God's redemptive plan.

The church's identity is not found in uniformity but in diverse unity around the Lamb. This challenges ethnocentric theology and cultural superiority. The people of God do not belong to any one nation—they are the citizens of a kingdom not built by human hands.

This vision also has profound implications for mission. The church is not an institution to be preserved but a people to be mobilized. It exists not to maintain power but to embody the Lamb's way of service, witness, and welcome. Mission is not conquest—it is participation in the healing of the nations, the end toward which Revelation moves (22:2).

Worshiping Communities in Context

Revelation's images of the church are both eschatological and immediate. They show what is true in God's eyes and what will one day be fully manifest. Around the world today, this community already sings, serves, and suffers—often in obscurity, but always in communion with the Lamb.

Pentecostal believers gathering before dawn in Nairobi, migrant farmworkers praying in Central America, Filipino Christians leading hymn festivals, Indigenous churches translating Scripture into their languages—these are glimpses of the multitude before the throne. Their songs, languages, and lives testify that the Lamb is gathering his people, and that the church of Jesus Christ cannot be confined to any one culture, form, or expression.

Yet Revelation also challenges churches that forget their calling. The church that aligns with empire, that ignores the oppressed, or that silences the voices of others risks losing its place in the Lamb's vision. To be the people of God is to follow the Lamb wherever he goes—into suffering, into mission, and into resurrection hope.

Questions for Reflection or Discussion
- How does Revelation's vision of the multiethnic, unified, worshiping people of God shape your understanding of Christian identity? What factors might hinder that from becoming a reality in your setting?
- In what ways can your own church embody the faithful endurance portrayed in Revelation 14 and 15?

Chapter 9
Babylon the Great and the Fall of Empire

Babylon as Imperial Power

In Revelation 17–18, the scene shifts to a vivid and devastating portrayal of Babylon the Great, a symbol of seductive and oppressive empire. Babylon is introduced as a woman "clothed in purple and scarlet… holding a golden cup full of abominations," seated on a scarlet beast with seven heads and ten horns (Rev. 17:3–5). She is described as "the great prostitute" and "the mother of whores and of earth's abominations." Her name is mystery: Babylon the Great.

This image echoes the Old Testament's portrayal of Babylon as the great oppressor of God's people (e.g., Isa. 47; Jer. 51). But in John's context, Babylon is a thinly veiled reference to Rome—the empire that ruled over the Mediterranean world with military might, economic dominance, and religious imperialism. The seven heads are "seven mountains" (17:9), almost certainly pointing to the seven hills of Rome. The language of seduction and violence captures how the empire both lured and crushed its subjects.

Yet Babylon is more than Rome. Like the beasts of Revelation 13, Babylon is a transhistorical symbol — a stand-in for any political, economic, or cultural system that exalts itself above God, exploits the vulnerable, and deceives the nations. Babylon is empire at its most seductive, dressed in luxury, drunk on blood, promising peace but built on violence.

John's vision unmasks empire's glittering facade. The woman appears regal, but her beauty is false. Her golden cup is filled with impurity. She rides the beast, but she is also devoured by it (17:16). The very systems that sustain her will ultimately betray her. The fall of Babylon is not only inevitable — it is divinely decreed.

Idolatry, Commerce, and Seduction

Revelation 18 portrays Babylon's fall as a moment of both judgment and exposure. An angel cries out,
> Fallen, fallen is Babylon the great! She has become a dwelling place of demons… (18:2).

The reasons for her fall are many: arrogance, exploitation, spiritual corruption, and above all, the commodification of human life. The list of goods traded by Babylon's merchants includes "gold, silver, jewels," and ends chillingly with "slaves — that is, human lives" (18:13).

This catalog of merchandise reveals that Babylon's sin is not only religious but economic. She thrives on luxury, markets the sacred, and treats people as things. She turns profit into idolatry and consumption into salvation. Her religion is consumerism, her liturgy is trade, and her altar is built on the backs of the poor.

The lament of the kings and merchants (18:9-19) is not for justice lost but for profits lost. They mourn not because Babylon was wicked, but because she was profitable. This reversal is Revelation's prophetic satire: those who worship wealth are shown to grieve its loss more than the lives crushed to gain it.

Babylon's seductive power lies in her ability to normalize injustice. She seduces not with tyranny alone, but with excess, entertainment, and comfort. This is what makes her so dangerous — her appeal is aesthetic, not merely coercive. She turns idolatry into spectacle, exploitation into luxury, and falsehood into common sense.

Prophetic Lament and Celebration

Into this scene of ruin comes a call from heaven:
> Come out of her, my people, so that you do not take part in her sins (18:4).

This summons is not simply physical but spiritual and ethical. The people of God are called to discernment, distance, and defiance. To come out of Babylon means to refuse her values, resist her narratives, and live as citizens of another kingdom. It is a call to holiness, not withdrawal; to prophetic imagination, not cultural captivity.

Then follows a double response: lament from the earth and rejoicing in heaven. Earth's kings and traders cry, "Alas, alas, the great city!" while heaven sings, "Rejoice over her, O heaven!" (18:19–20). These contrasting reactions reveal Revelation's moral polarity: what the world mourns, heaven celebrates; what the world admires, heaven condemns.

This is a liturgical moment—Revelation invites readers to join in heaven's perspective. Babylon's collapse is not only a political event but a theological one. It is the demolition of a false reality, the unveiling of a system built on lies. Her destruction clears the stage for the coming of the new Jerusalem (Rev. 21), a city not of domination, but of peace.

Global Readings of Empire and Resistance

Across history and geography, Revelation's portrayal of Babylon has found resonance in communities who have suffered under imperial oppression and economic injustice. African theologians have likened Babylon to colonial regimes that dehumanized and dispossessed. Latin American liberation theologians have read Babylon as neoliberal capitalism, which exploits labor, devastates the earth, and concentrates wealth in the hands of the few. Asian theologians have drawn attention to Babylon's religious pluralism manipulated by political powers.

In the Western world, Babylon has sometimes been misread as a future political entity, leading to sensationalized eschatologies. But Revelation is not interested in predicting a singular regime. It calls readers in every generation to identify the "Babylon" of their own context—whatever powers tempt the church with compromise, profit, or privilege.

Babylon still lives where wealth is worshiped, where the poor are expendable, where national power is mistaken for divine favor, and where truth is sacrificed for comfort. In such places, Revelation calls the church not to complicity, but to courageous resistance—rooted in worship, shaped by the cross, and animated by the hope of a better city.

Questions for Reflection or Discussion

- What forms do you think "Babylon" takes in today's world?

- What might it mean for Christians in your setting to hear the Spirit saying, "Come out of her (Babylon), my people" (Rev. 18:4)?
- How might the witness of Revelation challenge Christians to examine their everyday economic decisions?

Chapter 10
The Return of the King
Christ's Final Victory

The Rider on the White Horse (Rev. 19:11–16)

After the fall of Babylon, heaven erupts in celebration. "Hallelujah!" rings out across the heavens (Rev. 19:1–6), a rare word in the New Testament, used here to mark the joy of divine justice. Then John sees a dramatic vision:

> I saw heaven opened, and there was a white horse! Its rider is called Faithful and True… In righteousness he judges and makes war (19:11).

The rider is none other than Jesus Christ, portrayed not as the gentle teacher or the sacrificial Lamb—but as a warrior king. Yet this warrior's weapons and titles invite deeper reflection. His robe is already dipped in blood (19:13)—not the blood of his enemies, but likely his own, symbolizing the cross as the basis of his victory. His name is "The Word of God" (19:13), aligning him with the divine Logos of John's Gospel. From his mouth comes a sharp sword—indicating that his power is exercised through speech, truth, and judgment, not brute violence.

This paradoxical image blends triumph with sacrifice, power with humility. Christ rides forth not as a Caesar, but as one who conquers through self-giving love. He is "King of kings and Lord of lords" (19:16), and his appearance marks the decisive end of Babylon's counterfeit rule.

For the church, this vision is not a call to holy war but to faithful trust in the Lamb's justice. It assures persecuted communities that evil will not prevail and invites all disciples to align their hope not with worldly powers but with the One who reigns in righteousness.

The Binding of Satan and the Millennium (Rev. 20:1–6)

Following Christ's victorious appearance, Revelation 20 presents the controversial passage often referred to as the Millennium—a symbolic period of "a thousand years" during which Satan is bound and the faithful reign with Christ (20:1–6). Interpretations of this passage have varied widely throughout Christian history.

- Premillennial views interpret the thousand years as a future, literal reign of Christ on earth.
- Postmillennial perspectives see the millennium as a golden age of Christian influence leading up to Christ's return.

- Amillennial readings interpret the thousand years symbolically as the present reign of Christ through the church.

Rather than anchoring Revelation's meaning in a single timeline, this chapter calls us to focus on its theological purpose: Christ's authority has already triumphed over evil, and those who have suffered for his name are honored and raised to life. "They came to life and reigned with Christ a thousand years" (20:4). This vision affirms the vindication of the martyrs, the justice of God, and the ultimate defeat of Satan.

The "first resurrection" in this text symbolizes participation in Christ's victory now. It offers comfort to the persecuted and reminds the church that to suffer with Christ is to reign with him (cf. 2 Tim 2:12).

Final Judgment and the Book of Life (Rev. 20:7–15)

After the millennium, Satan is released for a final conflict. He deceives the nations once more, gathering them for battle—but fire from heaven consumes them, and the devil is cast into the lake of fire (20:7–10). This marks the end of evil's rebellion. It is not a dualistic standoff between equal forces—God's justice is never in doubt.

John then sees "a great white throne" (20:11). All the dead are judged "according to their works," and those whose names are not found in the "book of life" are thrown into the lake of fire (20:12-15). This sobering scene reminds us that human actions matter, that justice will be done, and that evil will not go unchecked.

Yet even here, judgment serves a redemptive purpose. The goal is not destruction for its own sake but the cleansing of creation from what defiles and destroys. The lake of fire is reserved not for flawed human beings who struggle in faith, but for unrepentant evil, empire, and the satanic logic of domination. Revelation holds these realities in tension: God's justice is real, and so is God's mercy.

The Lamb's Victory and the Vindication of the Saints

Revelation 19-20 is not a detached vision of the end times—it is a theological revelation of how Christ's future victory reframes the present. The faithful are not forgotten. Those who have suffered, died, or endured marginalization for Christ's name are honored, raised, and enthroned (20:4).

Throughout the book, the faithful are described not by titles of power, but by their relationship to the Lamb. They are those who "follow the Lamb wherever he goes" (14:4), who "keep the commandments of God and hold fast to the faith of Jesus" (14:12). They are the ones whose robes have been washed in the blood of the Lamb (7:14), and whose names are written in the Lamb's book of life (21:27).

This is not abstract hope — it is pastoral and political, especially for believers in contexts of persecution, economic exploitation, or systemic racism. The return of the King is not a threat but a promise: a pledge that justice will be done, truth will be revealed, and the humble will be lifted up.

Global Voices and Apocalyptic Hope

Across the globe, Revelation's vision of Christ's return has sustained communities facing trauma and oppression. In African-American spirituals, the refrain "King Jesus is listening" expresses both accountability and intimacy. For Christians in places of violence, poverty, or marginalization, the white horse and the crowned rider are not symbols of fear but of liberating hope. The imagery affirms that evil does not have the final word, and that God is not passive in the face of injustice.

At the same time, Revelation critiques triumphalist eschatologies that turn Christ's return into a justification for domination or indifference. The returning King is not Caesar redux. He is the

Lamb who was slain. His justice is restorative, his power is sacrificial, and his throne is built not on conquest but on the cross.

Questions for Reflection or Discussion
- Do you think that the church in your context takes Revelation's vision of Christ's return seriously enough? Why or why not?
- How might the anticipation of final justice shape how Christians live, practically?

Chapter 11
A New Heaven and New Earth

The New Jerusalem as God's Dwelling Place (Rev. 21:1-4)

As Revelation draws to a close, the curtain is lifted on the climactic vision of hope:

> Then I saw a new heaven and a new earth… And I saw the holy city, the New Jerusalem, coming down out of heaven from God (Rev. 21:1-2).

This vision marks a radical shift. The trajectory of the biblical story is not one of human souls escaping to heaven but of heaven coming to earth. God does not abandon creation; God redeems it. The holy city descends, not floats away. It is a vision of divine presence renewing the world from within.

At the center of this new creation is relationship:

> See, the home of God is among mortals… they will be his peoples, and God himself will be with them (21:3).

This intimate promise echoes the covenant refrain of the Hebrew Scriptures and fulfills the deepest longing of the human heart. Grief, death, and pain are no more (21:4). The former things have passed away—not by annihilation but by transformation.

Revelation does not end in destruction. It ends in communion.

The Reversal of the Fall and the Fulfillment of the Covenant

The New Jerusalem is not a literal city built of gold and jewels, but a symbolic reality that fulfills the promises of Scripture and reverses the curse of Genesis. In Eden, humanity was expelled from God's presence. In the New Jerusalem, God dwells permanently with creation. In Eden, the tree of life was guarded. In the New Jerusalem, it grows in the center of the city, accessible to all (22:2).

The architecture of the city is deeply theological. It is built on twelve foundations (21:14), representing the apostles, and has twelve gates (21:12), named after the tribes of Israel. Its dimensions—twelve thousand stadia in length, width, and height—form a perfect cube, echoing the Holy of Holies in the temple. The point is clear: the entire city is now the dwelling place of God. There is no temple because the whole of creation is sacred.

This is the telos of redemption—not disembodied escape, but embodied restoration. The nations are not abolished; they are healed (22:2). Culture is not erased; its glory is brought into the city (21:26). The sun and moon are not banished; they are surpassed by the radiance of God's presence (21:23).

The New Jerusalem fulfills the Abrahamic covenant (a land for all peoples), the Mosaic covenant (a just community), and the Davidic covenant (God's eternal reign through the Lamb). It is the ecclesiological and eschatological hope of the church—not just a place we long for, but a reality we begin to embody.

Healing of the Nations and Ecological Renewal

At the heart of the city flows the river of the water of life, flanked by the tree of life, bearing fruit each month and offering leaves "for the healing of the nations" (22:1–2). This is not poetic flourish—it is a theological proclamation: God's future includes creation's healing and humanity's reconciliation.

The tree of life, denied in Genesis, is now abundant. The river recalls the streams of Ezekiel's temple (Ezek. 47) and the living water of Jesus' promise (John 7:38). This is not a private paradise, but a communal ecosystem of healing—where violence is undone, estrangement overcome, and life shared.

This vision has profound implications for ecological theology. The future is not anti-material or anti-environmental. The Lamb's reign affirms the goodness of creation and its rightful flourishing. In a world threatened by environmental collapse and ecological injustice, Revelation 22 offers not despair but a sacramental vision of creation's restoration.

The Church as a Foretaste of the New Jerusalem

Though Revelation 21–22 points toward the future, it is not a distant fantasy. The church today is called to embody the reality of the New Jerusalem in the present. Just as the Lamb is already enthroned, the people of the Lamb are already a sign, sacrament, and foretaste of what is to come.

This means that Christian communities are to be places of welcome, healing, justice, and holiness—reflecting the character of the city whose architect is God. In every act of reconciliation, every word of truth, every meal shared in Christ's name, the church enacts the coming kingdom.

The call to "come out of Babylon" (18:4) is matched by the invitation to "enter the city" (22:14). This eschatological tension is the space in which the church lives. We are not yet home—but we are already citizens of the city to come (Phil. 3:20). Our lives are meant to anticipate and reflect that reality.

To be the church is to refuse despair, resist Babylon, and live as pilgrims and prophets of the coming new creation. We do not build the New Jerusalem, but we bear witness to it.

Eschatological Ethics: Living the Future Now

Revelation ends with a plea and a promise: "The Spirit and the bride say, 'Come'… Let anyone who is thirsty come (22:17)."

This is a word of mission and invitation. The church is not to hoard this vision but to extend it — offering living water to the thirsty and hope to the despairing. Eschatology is not an escape plan but a missional summons. We are called to live the future now — to embody the Lamb's reign in our practices of justice, worship, ecology, and community.

Revelation closes with longing: "Come, Lord Jesus!" (22:20). But even that longing is filled with assurance: "Surely I am coming soon."

Until then, we live in the in-between — already sealed, already sent, already beloved. The grace of the Lord Jesus is with us (22:21), and we walk forward not in fear, but in hope.

Questions for Reflection or Discussion

- How does the vision of the New Jerusalem shape your personal and communal sense of Christian hope?

- What practices might help the church live as a foretaste of the new creation promised in Revelation?
- What role might Revelation's vision of the New Jerusalem play in how Christians participate in the mission of God today?

Chapter 12
Some Leading Interpreters of Revelation

Why Interpretation Matters

Few biblical books demand as much interpretive care as the Book of Revelation. Its potent symbols and poetic resistance have inspired not only hope but also misuse — whether through fear-driven eschatology, rigid systems of prediction, or culturally captive readings. Yet throughout the history of the church, Revelation has also been a life-giving text, especially for communities in distress, calling readers to faithful witness and deep imagination.

This chapter introduces students to some leading interpreters of Revelation, drawn from early Christianity to the present. It highlights global, theological, and gender-diverse voices, showing how different lenses bring out different dimensions of the Apocalypse. Reading Revelation is not about finding the "correct" meaning, but entering into a communal conversation shaped by context, faith, and courage.

Early Church Voices
Irenaeus, Victorinus, and Tyconius

Irenaeus of Lyons (2nd century) was among the first theologians to affirm the apostolic authorship and authority of Revelation. He emphasized its eschatological hope and saw in it a defense against Gnostic dualism. Irenaeus's future-oriented, premillennial interpretation linked Revelation with the eventual defeat of evil through Christ's return.

Victorinus of Pettau (d. c. 304), author of the earliest known commentary on Revelation, offered an allegorical and anti-imperial reading. He saw Rome as the beast and emphasized the book's symbolic narrative. His commentary laid groundwork for the symbolic interpretations that would flourish in later centuries.

Tyconius, a 4th-century North African Donatist, offered an influential spiritual reading of Revelation, viewing its battles and judgments as an ongoing struggle within the church and the world. His work profoundly shaped later interpreters, including Augustine, and anticipated amillennial readings that saw Revelation as describing the church age rather than a future chronology. This way of reading Revelation helped move eschatology from speculative prediction to ethical formation and continues to influence Christian interpretation today.

Recent Interpreters of Revelation

Modern scholarship has opened new vistas for understanding Revelation's theology, literary structure, and socio-political implications. Among the most influential voices are the following:

Richard Bauckham, in *The Theology of the Book of Revelation*, presents Revelation as a literary and theological masterpiece rooted in Old Testament prophecy. He highlights the book's vision of universal worship, divine justice, and the subversive power of the slain Lamb. For Bauckham, Revelation is not just about the end of the world—it is about the unveiling of God's purposes in history and worship.

Craig R. Koester, in both *Revelation and the End of All Things* and his authoritative *Anchor Yale Bible Commentary* on Revelation (2014), offers a balanced reading that is deeply pastoral, literarily sensitive, and historically informed. His commentary highlights the book's cyclical structure, symbolic richness, and the deep theological challenge it poses to complacency. Koester's work helps the church recover Revelation as a word of comfort, challenge, and ultimate hope.

David Aune, whose three-volume commentary in the *Word Biblical Commentary* series is one of the most detailed available, offers a historical-critical analysis grounded in Greco-

Roman background and Jewish apocalyptic literature. He situates Revelation within its ancient literary context and helps modern readers appreciate its symbolic language and rhetorical strategy.

G. K. Beale, in his *New International Greek Testament Commentary* on Revelation, represents a Reformed theological lens and emphasizes symbolic and covenantal interpretations. Beale reads Revelation as a symbolic portrayal of the entire church age, stressing spiritual conflict and divine sovereignty. His work is rich in intertextual connections to the Old Testament and deeply ecclesiological in tone.

Brian K. Blount, in his Revelation volume for the *New Testament Library* series (2009), brings a Black theological and liberationist perspective to the Apocalypse. He interprets Revelation through the lens of African American experience, focusing on perseverance, resistance, and eschatological hope. Blount emphasizes Revelation's pastoral voice to suffering communities and its call to embodied prophetic witness in the face of empire and oppression.

These interpreters differ in method and emphasis, yet together they affirm Revelation as a text of profound theological vision, capable of speaking across times, cultures, and struggles.

Global Voices
Boesak, Pablo Richard, and Néstor Míguez

Allan Boesak, a South African Reformed pastor and anti-apartheid leader, reads Revelation as a manifesto of hope for the oppressed. In Babylon, Boesak saw apartheid; in the Lamb, the strength to resist. His sermons and writings emphasized God's preferential option for the poor and Revelation's call to faithful, risky resistance.

Pablo Richard (Chile), a Latin American liberation theologian, interprets Revelation in its ancient Roman context as a message of hope and resistance for oppressed communities. He emphasizes its critique of empire and its call for justice and social transformation. Rather than a prediction of future catastrophe, he sees Revelation as a prophetic text empowering believers to confront injustice and live in solidarity with the marginalized.

Néstor Míguez, an Argentine Methodist theologian, draws on the experiences of the Latin American church to interpret Revelation as a critique of economic exploitation and neoliberal capitalism. His work connects Revelation's imagery of Babylon and the beast with debt systems, poverty, and global inequality. The New Jerusalem, for Míguez, represents solidarity, justice, and the dignity of the poor.

These global voices remind readers that Revelation speaks not only from the margins but to the margins, offering apocalyptic vision as a lens of resistance, healing, and transformation.

Female Scholars and Feminist Perspectives

Elisabeth Schüssler Fiorenza, in *The Book of Revelation: Justice and Judgment*, foregrounds Revelation as a document of resistance produced by a marginalized community under imperial pressure. She critiques readings that celebrate violent imagery without considering its rhetorical and political context. Fiorenza's work has profoundly shaped feminist biblical interpretation and insists that justice — not spectacle — is Revelation's theological center.

Catherine Keller, a constructive theologian, reclaims Revelation for ecological and political imagination. In her most recent work, *Facing Apocalypse: Climate, Democracy, and Other Last Chances* (2021), Keller critiques apocalyptic dualism and determinism, calling instead for relational eschatology and open futures. She sees in Revelation both danger and promise — a narrative that can feed both dystopia and hopeful resistance, depending on how it is read and enacted.

Barbara Rossing, in *The Rapture Exposed: The Message of Hope in the Book of Revelation*, offers a popular-level yet theologically rich engagement with Revelation. She dismantles dispensationalist eschatologies and recovers Revelation as a vision of nonviolent hope and ecological renewal. Rossing reads the Lamb not as a warrior but as a sign of divine vulnerability, challenging militarized readings and affirming God's healing purposes for the world.

These feminist theologians offer critical correctives and constructive insights. They help the church read Revelation in ways that are faithful to the Lamb, inclusive of women's experiences, and attentive to justice, ecology, and liberation.

Toward a Polyphonic Reading of Revelation

What emerges from this chapter is a polyphonic theology of Revelation. No single voice is sufficient; each lens—historical, literary, theological, contextual—contributes a vital perspective. Whether in the academy, the pulpit, or grassroots communities, interpretation is never neutral. It either reinforces empire or resists it. It either narrows the Lamb's vision or amplifies it.

To interpret Revelation faithfully is to listen carefully—to the text, to the Spirit, and to the voices of those who have found in its pages both fire and light. The book is not merely about the end. It is about enduring in the present with a vision of the Lamb's future. Through these interpreters, the church is invited to read Revelation with reverence, urgency, and hope.

Questions for Reflection or Discussion
- How have different historical and cultural contexts shaped how Revelation has been interpreted?
- Which interpreter(s) introduced in this chapter resonate most with your understanding or raise new questions for you?
- What can global and female interpreters teach us about reading Revelation today?

Chapter 13
Preaching and Teaching Revelation Today

Introduction
Why Preach Revelation?

For many preachers and teachers, the Book of Revelation is as intimidating as it is captivating. Its dragons, beasts, cosmic battles, and cryptic numbers have led some to avoid it entirely, while others wield it as a tool of fear or control. Yet Revelation is part of the canon, given to the church not to confuse or terrify, but to inspire faithfulness, ignite hope, and call communities to live as witnesses of the Lamb.

Preaching and teaching Revelation is not optional—it is vital. Especially in a world marked by empire, ecological collapse, war, and injustice, Revelation reminds the church of its true identity and future. But to engage it faithfully, one must approach it with humility, care, theological depth, and pastoral sensitivity.

The Pastoral Purpose of Revelation

At its core, Revelation is a pastoral letter—written to real churches facing persecution, compromise, and marginalization. Its author, John, does not seek to satisfy curiosity about the end times but to nurture endurance and hope in the present. Preachers and teachers must therefore begin with the book's pastoral heart.

John addresses seven churches (Rev. 2-3), each with unique struggles: apathy, fear, sexual immorality, doctrinal confusion, and political compromise. Today's congregations face similar challenges. Revelation provides a framework for honest reflection, calling churches to renewed vision, repentance, and faithfulness.

The genre of apocalypse serves a pastoral function: it pulls back the veil to show reality from God's perspective. It confronts complacency, unmasks empire, and empowers communities to stand firm amid suffering. Good preaching and teaching will preserve this prophetic and pastoral edge.

Key Themes to Emphasize

Effective teaching of Revelation focuses not on speculation but on theological clarity. Among the most important themes to communicate are:

The Centrality of the Lamb

At every turn, the slain yet standing Lamb (Rev. 5:6) remains the focal point. Christ is not only the Savior but also the model for discipleship (Rev. 14:4). All power in Revelation is redefined through the cross. Teaching must emphasize that the way of the Lamb is nonviolent, sacrificial, and victorious in weakness.

Worship as Resistance

Revelation is filled with hymns, doxologies, and visions of cosmic worship. Worship is not escapism—it is resistance to Babylon. Teaching Revelation should help congregations see their worship as political, prophetic, and participatory in God's reign.

Judgment as Justice

Rather than fear-mongering, Revelation's judgment scenes should be framed as God's commitment to justice. Babylon's fall is the liberation of the oppressed. Teaching must show that judgment flows from God's holiness and is oriented toward the renewal of creation.

The New Creation as Hope

Revelation ends not in destruction but in renewal—a new heaven and earth, a garden-city where God dwells with humanity. Preaching must present Revelation's eschatology not as escape from the world, but as the healing of the world.

Teaching Revelation in a Global Context

Teaching Revelation globally demands attention to contextual and cultural nuance. In many parts of the world, Revelation resonates deeply with communities facing political oppression, poverty, war, or ecological degradation. The imagery of Babylon, the beast, and the New Jerusalem speaks with prophetic power.

At the same time, Revelation has been misused—weaponized to support colonial agendas, promote rapture-based escapism, or fuel anti-Semitic and Islamophobic ideas. Teachers must be vigilant in deconstructing harmful readings and emphasizing the book's radical inclusivity, critique of empire, and theological depth.

Drawing from global and diverse interpreters (see Chapter 12) allows for a richer, more faithful pedagogy. Examples from liberation theology, African and Asian contexts, Indigenous experience, and feminist critiques ensure that Revelation is taught as a text for the whole church—not just one tradition or geography.

Homiletical Strategies for Preaching Revelation

Avoid Speculation; Preach Christ.

Do not reduce Revelation to timelines, charts, or predictions. Keep Christ at the center, especially as the slain Lamb.

Preach the Text, Not Just the Symbols.

Let the text speak. Focus on its structure, imagery, and theological flow. Avoid over-allegorizing or flattening the poetry.

Name the Powers

Babylon is not just Rome. It lives wherever power is abused and idolatry is normalized. Faithful preaching will help communities discern and resist today's empires.

Use Liturgy and Imagination

Revelation is filled with songs, prayers, and visions. Use liturgical creativity — art, music, and visual symbolism — to make the text come alive.

Preach Hope Boldly

Above all, Revelation is about hope — not cheap optimism, but apocalyptic hope rooted in God's faithfulness. It tells the truth about the world's suffering and insists that the Lamb will have the last word.

Teaching in the Classroom
Recommendations for Instructors

Start with Context

Ground students in the historical setting of the first-century Roman Empire and the situation of the seven churches.

Highlight Genre Awareness

Teach how apocalyptic literature functions. Discuss symbolism, visions, and prophetic critique.

Use Diverse Voices

Include scholarship and testimonies from around the world, especially voices from marginalized communities.

Encourage Ethical Reflection

Prompt students to ask: What does it mean to live as citizens of the New Jerusalem today? What does "coming out of Babylon" require of us?

Balance Theology and Pastoral Care

Help students see how to teach Revelation in ways that are theologically robust and pastorally sensitive.

Conclusion
Living and Teaching the Apocalypse

Revelation ends with an invitation: "The Spirit and the bride say, 'Come!'" (Rev. 22:17) and a promise: "Surely I am coming soon." (22:20)

Preaching and teaching Revelation is a sacred calling. It is not about predicting the future but proclaiming the Lamb, nurturing resilient hope, and calling the church to live now as a foretaste of the world to come.

May those who teach and preach Revelation do so with courage, creativity, and compassion—helping the church to see not just what is, but what must soon take place (Rev. 1:1), and to follow the Lamb wherever he goes (14:4).

Questions for Reflection or Discussion

- What challenges and opportunities do you anticipate in preaching or teaching Revelation in your own context?
- How can the book of Revelation become a resource of encouragement and imagination rather than fear or confusion?
- What are some practical ways you might apply some of the homiletical and teaching strategies listed in this chapter in your local church context?

Epilogue
Living Revelation Today

The Book of Revelation is not merely a record of ancient visions or a roadmap to the future. It is a living word—calling the church in every time and place to discern, to worship, and to follow the Lamb. In a world still marked by empire, injustice, and suffering, Revelation awakens our theological imagination and moral courage. It dares us to see history not through fear or cynicism, but through the lens of God's faithfulness and the Lamb's victory.

This book has sought to accompany readers on a journey of faithful engagement with Revelation—through careful interpretation, global perspectives, and a posture of worship and hope. Yet the true work of interpretation continues in the life of the church: in its preaching and teaching, in its resistance to injustice, and in its witness to the coming kingdom.

As students, pastors, and communities continue to listen to what the Spirit is saying to the churches, may they do so with reverence, joy, and courage. For the Lamb who was slain is alive. The New Jerusalem is coming. And the church is called

to be a sign, a song, and a servant of that promise—
until God makes all things new.

Selected Bibliography

Aune, David E. 1997-1998. *Revelation*. Word Biblical Commentary, 3 vols. Dallas: Word Books; Nashville: Thomas Nelson.

Bauckham, Richard. 1993. *The Climax of Prophecy: Studies on the Book of Revelation*. Edinburgh: T&T Clark.

Bauckham, Richard. 1993. *The Theology of the Book of Revelation*. Cambridge: Cambridge University Press.

Beale, G. K. 1999. *The Book of Revelation: A Commentary on the Greek Text*. New International Greek Testament Commentary. Grand Rapids: Eerdmans.

Blount, Brian K. 2005. *Can I Get a Witness? Reading Revelation through African American Culture*. Louisville: Westminster John Knox.

Blount, Brian K. 2009. *Revelation: A Commentary*. New Testament Library. Louisville: Westminster John Knox.

Boesak, Allan A. 1987. *Comfort and Protest: Reflections on the Apocalypse of John of Patmos*. Louisville: Westminster John Knox.

Fiorenza, Elisabeth Schüssler. 1991. *Revelation: Vision of a Just World*. Minneapolis: Fortress Press.

Flemming, Dean. 2022. *Foretaste of the Future: Reading Revelation in Light of God's Mission*. Downers Grove, IL: IVP Academic.

Gorman, Michael J. 2011. *Reading Revelation Responsibly: Uncivil Worship and Witness, Following the Lamb into the New Creation*. Eugene, OR: Cascade Books.

Gwyther, Timothy, and Wes Howard-Brook. 1999. *Unveiling Empire: Reading Revelation Then and Now*. Maryknoll, NY: Orbis Books.

Keller, Catherine. 2021. *Facing Apocalypse: Climate, Democracy, and Other Last Chances*. Maryknoll, NY: Orbis Books.

Koester, Craig R. 2014. *Revelation: A New Translation with Introduction and Commentary*. Anchor Yale Bible, vol. 38A. New Haven: Yale University Press.

_____. 2018. *Revelation and the End of All Things*. 2nd ed. Grand Rapids: Eerdmans.

McKnight, Scot, and Cody Matchett. 2023. *Revelation for the Rest of Us: A Prophetic Call to Follow Jesus as a Dissident Disciple*. Grand Rapids: Zondervan.

Míguez, Néstor. 1995. "Revelation and the Victims of Economic Exclusion: Reading Revelation 18 from a Latin American Context." In *Reading from This Place: Social Location and Biblical Interpretation in Global Perspective*, edited by Fernando F. Segovia and Mary Ann Tolbert, 135–150. Minneapolis: Fortress Press.

Paul, Ian. *Revelation*. 2018. Tyndale New Testament Commentaries. Downers Grove: IL/ London, IVP Academic.

Reddish, Mitchell. 2001. *Revelation*. Smyth and Helwys Bible Commentary. Macon, GA: Smyth and Helwys.

Rhoads, David, ed. 2005. *From Every People and Nation: The Book of Revelation in Intercultural Perspective*. Minneapolis: Fortress Press.

Richard, Pablo. 2009. *Apocalypse: A People's Commentary on the Book of Revelation*. Eugene, OR: Wipf and Stock.

Rossing, Barbara R. 2004. *The Rapture Exposed: The Message of Hope in the Book of Revelation*. Boulder, CO: Westview Press.

Thomas, John Christopher and Frank D. Macchia. *Revelation*. The Two Horizons New Testament Commentary. Grand Rapids, Eerdmans, 2016.

Thompson, Leonard L. 1990. *The Book of Revelation: Apocalypse and Empire*. New York: Oxford University Press.

Weinrich, William C., ed. *Revelation*. Ancient Christian Commentary on Scripture. Downers Grove, IL: IVP Academic, 2005.

Wright, N. T. 2011. *Revelation for Everyone*. London: SPCK.

Appendix

Locating the Seven Churches of Ancient Asia Minor in their Contemporary Setting

The churches were located in modern Turkey, north of the Mediterranean Sea between Europe and Asia.

The churches were located in the Western part of Turkey. Maps generated by AI.

www.ingramcontent.com/pod-product-compliance
Lightning Source LLC
LaVergne TN
LVHW021400080426
835508LV00020B/2377